Emma—

Once again, God's plan resulted in a perfect little girl coming to an incredible family!! We wish you a life of good health, many giggles & laughter and love! We are so glad you are part of our lives!

Love,

The Perentis Family

OUR KIDSPAK™

JORJAK   MARISAK   RATAK   PATTIWAK

"A" is for ADOPTED

by Eileen Tucker Cosby

illustrated by Norma S. Strange

SWAK Pak, LLC

SWAK Pak, LLC

Text ©2000 by Eileen Tucker Cosby
Illustrated ©2000 by Norma S. Strange

Job No. SWA-001.

First Edition

ISBN 0-9676385-0-X
Library of Congress Card Number: 00-192246

This book is dedicated to:

a loving and awesome **God**;

my wonderful and dedicated husband, **David**;

my outstanding parents, **Tommie and Mary Tucker**;

all adopted children everywhere and their parents;

all birthmothers who proved their love for their children by placing them for adoption;

and my gift from **God**, my son, **Jordan**.

A special thank you to **Donna Davis**, **Norma Strange**, **Jo-an Holstein**, **Jo Cook**
and a host of friends and relatives who supported the efforts of publishing this book.
We especially want to thank **Ken and Sharon Nelson** for sharing
our vision and helping to make our dream come true.

a

adopted

A special woman who loves you very much carried you inside her tummy while you grew. When you were born, she chose a special Mommy and Daddy, who also love you very much, to take care of you.

"A" is for adopted.

You were chosen from the start

To be loved, nurtured and cherished from the bottom of our hearts.

We're proud to be your parents. We're very proud of you.

We hope that this adoption makes you as proud too!

b

beautiful

You are the most beautiful person we have ever seen. We have loved you from the moment we first saw your sweet little face and tiny little toes.

Beautiful like the sunset; beautiful like a flower

From the moment you came into lives

You are more beautiful every hour.

cuddle

Cuddling with you
will always be one of our
favorite things to do.

We want to hold you
close so you can hear our
hearts beat next to yours.

Let's cuddle
in the morning.

Let's cuddle
in the night.

Let's cuddle
in the noon
time hour.

Let's cuddle
all our lives.

daddy

Daddy couldn't wait to bring you home. He loves to hold you in his arms and play with you. Your Daddy has great plans for you. He is so happy he adopted you!

Daddy is someone you love to have around.

He plays peek-a-boo and makes funny animal sounds.

He'll always be there for you, in everything you do.

And nothing can take away the love he feels for you.

e excited

We were so happy when we learned that you were going to be part of our family! Ever since that day, we have been excited to have you with us and watch you grow.

The phone rang, and then we knew.

Our dream came true;
our baby would be you!

We couldn't wait to
hold you in our hands.

Immediately we made
our plans

To bring home our
baby right away.

Oh what an
unforgettable day!

family

You have many family members who love you. You are also special to our friends. You have little friends, big friends and animal friends. You make many people happy!

Your family and friends are special
people to run with, jump and play

To be there when you need them,
no matter what time of day.

If you ever feel sad and lonely,
and need someone to care,

Your family and friends are always there,
with lots of love
to spare.

g

grandparents

Your Grandparents are very proud of you. They know you are beautiful, smart and wonderful.

Grandmom and Granddad
think you're the best.

You bring them so much
laughter and happiness.

They like to pinch your cheeks
and tickle your feet.

And give you lots of hugs and kisses
because you are so sweet.

Heavenly Father

Our Heavenly Father, the creator of every living thing, answered our prayers when we asked for you. We thank Him every day for choosing us to be your parents, and for choosing you to be our child.

One day the heavens opened and showered us with you.

Our Heavenly Father did as He promised and made our dream come true.

He chose us to discipline, guide, and love you tenderly.

He chose you to be obedient, to grow and to flourish in our faithful family.

inspiration

Being with you inspires us
to be loving parents, better
children to our parents, and
closer to our friends. Thank
you for your inspiration.

i

You are the inspiration that makes our lives complete.

You are the inspiration that celebrates victory, not defeat.

You are the inspiration that guides us through each day.

You are our inspiration; we love you more than words can say.

joy

Since you came into our lives,
our hearts are filled with joy.
We are happy. We are blessed.
We are joyful!

J

Joy is a feeling of
happiness and bliss.

It is hard to explain a
feeling such as this.

It's a feeling reaching
down to the bottom
of our hearts.

And it lets us know
without a doubt,
we will never part.

k

kiss

Kissing you is just one way to show our love for you. We love to kiss you and kiss you and kiss you! We love you so much!

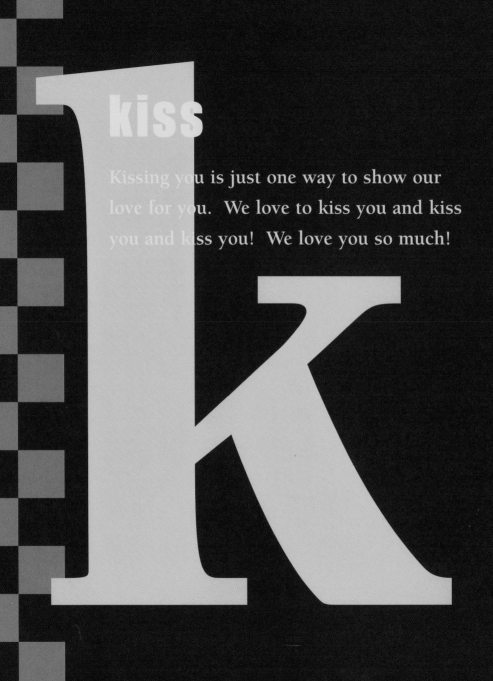

When we
see your rosy
cheeks and face
so sweet

We kiss you all over,
right down to your feet.

We kiss you at work.
We kiss you at play.

Our greatest joy
is kissing you
every day.

1 love

Loving you so
deeply makes
us understand
how special it
feels to be
loved. This
love between
us makes our
family happy
and strong.

We love you more than ice cream.

We love you more than pie.

We'll love you from now until eternity.

We'll love you all of our lives.

mommy

Your Mommy has loved you from the moment she laid eyes on you. She thanks God for you every time she holds you close and looks into your eyes. Just talking about you lights up Mommy's face.

Mommy loves to kiss you from your head to your toes.

She loves to play hide-and-seek and take you everywhere she goes.

At night, she reads you stories and sings sweet lullabies.

Just the thought of you brings tears of happiness to her eyes.

Aaron
Dave
Jordan
Ashley
Adrian
Heather
Brently
Anthony
Benjamin
Nicky
Aric
BethEl
Mary

n name

You were given a name that has great
meaning in your life. Your name is
how you will be identified by others,
and cherished by us.

Tommie

Parker

Rosie

Johnnie

Megan Ty

Alexys

Kiley

Marcus

Joey

Treyson

Elizabeth

Tarzan Vanessa

Julia

Your name was
chosen carefully
because you
are so loved.

It's a name that
fits you perfectly.
It fits you like
a glove.

When your name
is spoken, warm
feelings come
to mind

A reminder to
thank God for
being so loving
and kind.

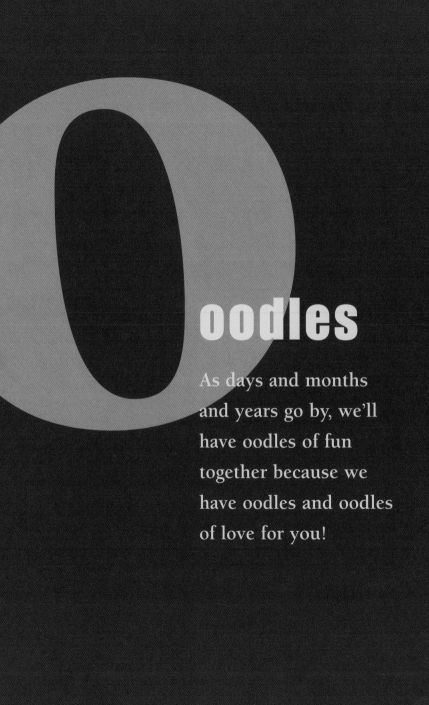

Oodles

As days and months
and years go by, we'll
have oodles of fun
together because we
have oodles and oodles
of love for you!

"Oodles" is a word,

One of the funniest words
we've ever heard.

But let there be no doubt

From top to bottom, inside and out

The whole kit and caboodles,

We love you oodles!

precious

When people ask us how you are, "precious" is the answer that always comes to mind with a smile.

p

You are more precious than
emeralds, diamonds, or pearls

More precious than any jewel
created in this world.

Many things are precious;
some are big and some are small.

Your Mommy and Daddy think you
are the most precious of all.

quiet

After a busy day, we cherish the quiet times we have with you. During these special moments, we think about how truly blessed we are.

In the quiet of the night,
when we lay you down to sleep

The peaceful feeling of the moment,
we pray the Lord will keep.

During this quiet time
we whisper in your ear

"Sleep well our little angel,
Mommy and Daddy
are near."

roar

You fill our lives and our hearts with such happiness. Every day we want to shout from the mountaintops and tell the world we love you!

Proud like the lion,
we want to roar

Because you're with
us forever more.

Your days ahead are
sunny and bright.

Let's fill each one
with great delight.

special

We fit together naturally as a family.
You were meant for us, and we were meant
for you. Our relationship is so special.

You are very special,
a child of many talents,
hopes and dreams.

Your glorious face and
radiant smile shine like
morning sunbeams.

You are very special.
You were created from
up above

To make a difference in
the world with your
kindness and your love.

thankful

We are truly thankful
to God for having you in
our lives. Thank you, God.

t

At the beginning of each day when we say to you, "Good morning,"

We take a moment to thank God by giving Him praises and glory.

We thank you, God, for this precious child and for our happy family.

Blessed be your name forever, we thank you Lord God Almighty.

unbelievable

We wanted a baby for so
long. When you finally
came into our lives, we
were unbelievably happy!

What do you say when your
dream finally comes true?

We're so delighted.
We just don't
know what to do!

The feeling that we have
is very hard to describe.

It's unbelievable!
At last you're here
by our side!

V

victory

As a family, we look forward to many adventures ahead. Learning new things, seeing new places and meeting new challenges will be the victories we share together.

Our family is like
a winning team,

Never giving up,
as hard as it
may seem.

We're going
for a victory.

We're making
family history!

And what's
the final score?

It's you who
we adore!

W

wonderful

It's wonderful to know we were picked by God to love you forever, no matter what. You are wonderful!

How can we explain the warm feeling inside?

A feeling so wonderful, it cannot be denied.

It's love for you, and it comes from deep within our souls.

Being your Mommy and Daddy are our most important roles.

xtra ordinary

We are so amazed at every word you say and move you make. You are unique. You are xtra-ordinary.

You are xtra-ordinary;
so beautiful in every way.

We want to tell the world
about you. There's so
much we want to say.

To put it very simply,
we're the happiest
parents on earth.

And that is why we
celebrate your extra
special birth.

y

yahoo

One way to show how excited we are to have you in our lives is to shout "yahoo!"

"Yahoo" is a funny word that means great joy.

It explains the love felt for every adopted girl and boy.

"Yahoo" expresses happiness for all you learn to do.

It's a thrill to watch you grow. Yahoo, yahoo, yahoo!

Z
zest

You have
such a zest
for life! You
light up any
room with
your smile
and energy.

You bring such joy to everyone you meet.

Your zest for life knocks us off our feet.

We're at the end of the alphabet now. It's time to say "goodnight."

May God be with you forever, and never let you out of sight.

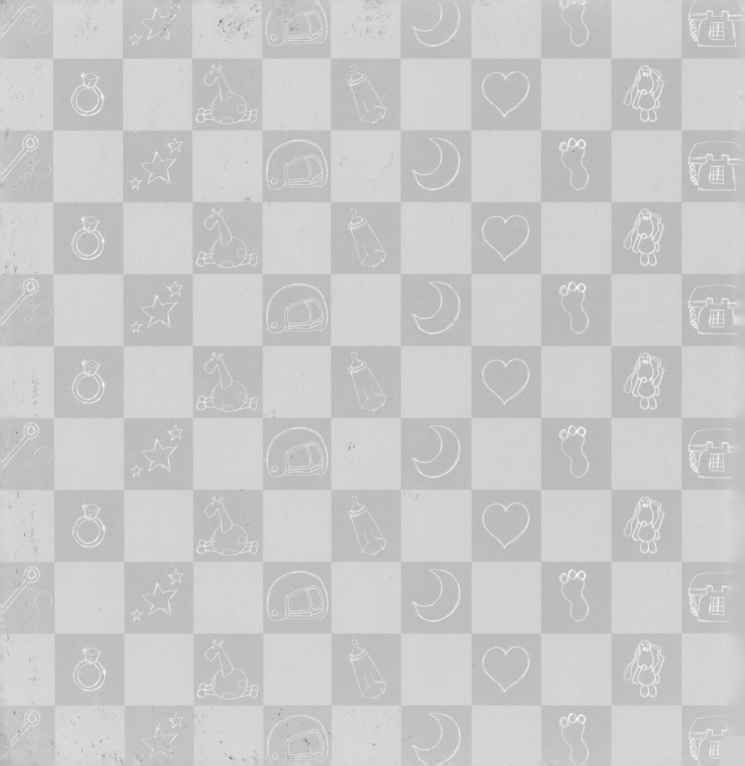